THIS WALKER BOOK BELONGS TO:

Bessie Coleman

"Brave Bessie"

was the name people gave to the young pilot Bessie Coleman back in the 1920s, when she flew as a daredevil stunt flyer in air shows all over the United States. Born in 1892, the daughter of a Native American father and an African-American mother, she grew up at a time when it was difficult for any woman to become a pilot, but for a black woman it seemed impossible. All the same, Bessie followed her dream and in 1921 she became the first licensed black aviator in the world.

To the family of Bessie Coleman,
with admiration and respect
from another flying family
R. L.

For my darling Richard
P. P.

Grateful acknowledgement and warm thanks above all to
Phil Hart, who remembered to tell the stories,
and to the memory of Professor George Bass of Brown
University, who never forgot the songs.
Finally, infinite affection to my editor and dear friend,
Amy Ehrlich, who from the very beginning has
believed in the Bessie Coleman story, and in this poem.
R. L.

First published 1996 by Walker Books Ltd
87 Vauxhall Walk, London SE11 5HJ

This edition published 1997

Text © 1996 Reeve Lindbergh
Illustrations © 1996 Pamela Paparone

10 9 8 7 6 5 4 3 2 1

Printed in Hong Kong

This book has been typeset in Usherwood.

British Library Cataloguing in Publication Data
A catalogue record for this book is available from
the British Library.

ISBN 0-7445-5412-8

THE STORY OF "BRAVE BESSIE" COLEMAN

Nobody Owns the Sky

Written by
Reeve Lindbergh

Illustrated by
Pamela Paparone

WALKER BOOKS
AND SUBSIDIARIES
LONDON • BOSTON • SYDNEY

There was a young woman who wanted to fly,

But the people said, "Kiss *that* wish good-bye!

The sky's too big and the sky's too high,

And you never will fly, so you'd better not try."

But this woman laughed, and she just said, "Why?

Nobody owns the sky!"

Up above flew the dove, and the raven too,

With the redbirds red and the bluebirds blue

And the brown hawks circling, far and few,

And the call of the swallows that follow the dew

When the high wild geese come travelling through

With the wind on their wings, flying free, flying true.

She called to them all, and she said, "Hey, you!

I'm coming up there, too!"

Bessie Coleman grew up a century ago

In a cabin built near where the creek waters flow.

She worked picking cotton, as white as the snow,

And watched cottony clouds up above come and go.

Bessie wished she could rise up and fly, high and low,

Over Texas, a long time ago.

Bessie's mother had not learned to read or to write,

But her children were raised to be eager and bright.

Bessie worked hard at school, and she dreamed about flight.

People said she was crazy; it wouldn't be right.

"You're a girl, not a man, and you're not even white!"

But did she stop dreaming? Not quite!

She went off to college and wanted to stay,

But it cost so much money that she couldn't pay.

She moved to Chicago and worked every day

At the White Sox barber shop, earning her way.

"White men can fly. Why can't I?" she would say,

But the flying schools turned her away.

Bessie manicured nails while the barber cut hair,

And she dreamed about flying, but didn't know where.

Then one day someone said, "Fly in France! They won't care

That you're black, and a woman." So Bessie went there.

She was young, tough, and smart, she had courage to spare,

And she took like a hawk to the air.

Bessie came home a pilot, so happy and proud!

She could ride on the wind, glide and spin in a cloud,

Parachute, loop-the-loop ... Bessie drew a huge crowd.

When she flew over airports or fields barely ploughed,

Her courage and daring had everyone wowed.

"Brave Bessie!" they shouted out loud.

On the ground Bessie lectured to crowds big and small –

People gathered in church, or inside the town hall.

"Come and fly, boys and girls! Black or white, short or tall,

Come and fly, everybody! Come, answer my call –

The air has no barrier, boundary, or wall.

The blue sky has room for us all."

Bessie's life was not long, but she flew far and wide.

In Chicago she showed off a Richthofen Glide,

Her air shows in Boston left crowds starry-eyed;

But in Jacksonville, Florida, everyone cried ...

Because Bessie's plane failed, and she fell, and she died.

"Farewell to Brave Bessie!" they sighed.

Other young men and women soon wanted to fly,

And the people said, "Why don't you give it a try?

The sky's still big, and the sky's still high,

But you're bound to get there, by and by.

Just remember her words till the day you die –

'*Nobody owns the sky!*'"

Look above, see the dove, and the raven too,

With the redbirds red and the bluebirds blue

And the brown hawks circling, far and few,

And the call of the swallows that follow the dew

When the high wild geese come travelling through

With the wind on their wings, flying free, flying true.

You can call to them all, you can say, "Hey, you!

I'm coming up there, too!"

MORE WALKER PAPERBACKS
For You to Enjoy

WHAT IS THE SUN?
by Reeve Lindbergh/Stephen Lambert

"A book of lasting distinction. Neatly skilled, simple verse, allied perfectly to Stephen Lambert's sensitive artwork… There is much to be learned here about the natural world." *Books for Keeps*

0-7445-4312-6   £3.99

NO PROBLEM
by Eileen Browne/David Parkins

Mouse is sure she can put together Rat's construction kit – NO problem!
But as she – and her friends – soon discover, it's not as simple as it seems!
The book includes a cut-out model plane to make.

"A fascinating and vividly illustrated story." *Books for Your Children*

0-7445-3632-4   £4.99

JAMAICA LOUISE JAMES
by Amy Hest/Sheila White Samton

Jamaica Louise James lives in New York with her Mama and Grammy.
She loves to draw and tell stories about the things she sees around her.
This colourful story tells of her big, cool idea for brightening up Grammy's birthday.

0-7445-5293-1   £4.99